W9-AJO-206

WITHDRAWN

Rookie
Read-About® Math

Making Change at the Fair

By Julie Dalton

Consultants
Chalice Bennett
Elementary Specialist
Martin Luther King Jr. Laboratory School
Evanston, Illinois

Ari Ginsburg
Math Curriculum Specialist

Children's Press®
A Division of Scholastic Inc.
New York   Toronto   London   Auckland   Sydney
Mexico City   New Delhi   Hong Kong
Danbury, Connecticut

Designer: Herman Adler Design
Photo Researcher: Caroline Anderson
The photo on the cover shows a student selling snacks at a school fair.

Library of Congress Cataloging-in-Publication Data

Dalton, Julie, 1951-
  Making change at the fair / by Julie Dalton.
      p. cm. — (Rookie read-about math)
   ISBN 0-516-24960-6 (lib. bdg.)   0-516-21224-9 (pbk.)
   1.   Counting—Juvenile literature. 2.   Money—Juvenile literature.
I. Title. II. Series.
   QA113.D3576 2006
   513.2'11—dc22
                                                                2005024299

Mr. Lee's class wants to earn money for a class trip. They will sell snacks at the school fair.

The children learn how to make change.

Mr. Lee says that making change is as easy as 1, 2, 3.

1. Say the amount you are given.
2. Say the cost of the item.
3. Count out coins to get to the amount you were given.

How to make change

- Say the amount you are given
- Say the cost of the item.
- Count out coins to get to the amount you were given.

The children practice
how to make change.
They know the value of
each coin.

A penny is 1 cent.
A nickel is 5 cents.
A dime is 10 cents.
A quarter is 25 cents.

Today is the day of the school fair!

The children will sell snacks. People will give them money. The children will make change.

10

A girl wants to buy a cup of popcorn.

A cup of popcorn costs 8 cents.

The girl gives Seth a dime. Seth knows that a dime equals 10 cents.

Now Seth must give the girl her change.

First, Seth says the amount he was given. "Ten cents," he says.

Next, he says the price of the popcorn, "Eight cents."

POPCORN
8¢

13

14

Seth starts at 8 cents and counts up to 10 cents.

He gives the girl a penny and says, "Nine cents." Then he gives her another penny and says, "Ten cents."

The girl's change is 2 cents.

A father wants to buy carrots. A cup of carrots costs 19 cents.

The father gives Allie a quarter.

Allie knows that a quarter equals 25 cents.

POPCORN

CARROTS
19¢

Now Allie must give the father his change.

First, Allie says the amount she was given. "Twenty-five cents," she says.

Next, she says the price of the carrots. "Nineteen cents," she says.

Allie counts up from
19 cents to 25 cents.

She gives the father a
penny and says, "Twenty
cents." Then she gives the
father a nickel and says,
"Twenty-five cents."

One penny plus one nickel
is 6 cents. The father's
change is 6 cents.

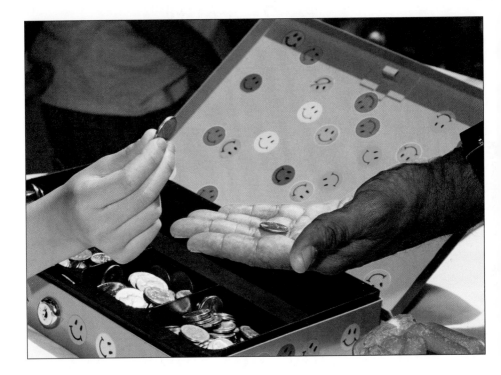

A woman wants to buy
an apple. An apple costs
29 cents.

The woman gives Matt
and Sara two quarters.

Matt and Sara know
that two quarters equal
50 cents.

Now the children
must give the woman
her change.

First, Sara says the
amount she was given.
"Fifty cents," she says.

Next, she says the
price of the apple,
"Twenty-nine cents."

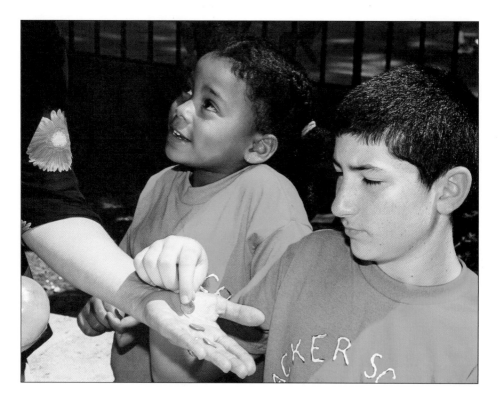

Matt gives the woman
a penny and says,
"Thirty cents."

Then he gives her a dime
and says, "Forty cents."

Then he gives her
another dime and says,
"Fifty cents."

The woman's change is
21 cents.

The fair has ended.

The children count the money they earned.

Hooray! They earned enough money for the class trip!

29

Words You Know

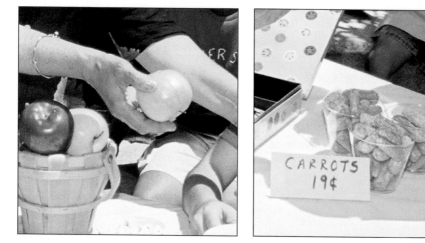

apple

carrots

change

coin

30

fair

popcorn

snacks

31

Index

About the Author

Julie Dalton is an editor and writer who lives in central Connecticut. She lives with her big hairy dog, a gentle cat, and several teenagers.

Photo Credits

All photographs copyright © 2006 Randy Matusow